Dogs

Border Collies

by Rebecca Stromstad Glaser

Consulting Editor: Gail Saunders-Smith, PhD

Consultant: Jennifer Zablotny, DVM
Member, American Veterinary Medical Association

Capstone
press
Mankato, Minnesota

Pebble Books are published by Capstone Press,
151 Good Counsel Drive, P.O. Box 669, Mankato, Minnesota 56002.
www.capstonepress.com

1 2 3 4 5 6 11 10 09 08 07 06

Library of Congress Cataloging-in-Publication Data
Glaser, Rebecca Stromstad.
    Border collies / by Rebecca Stromstad Glaser.
    p. cm.—(Pebble Books. Dogs)
    "Simple text and photographs present an introduction to the border collie breed,
its growth from puppy to adult, and pet care information"—Provided by publisher.
    Includes bibliographical references and index.
    ISBN-13: 978-0-7368-5331-6 (hardcover)
    ISBN-10: 0-7368-5331-6 (hardcover)
    1. Border collie—Juvenile literature. I. Title. II. Series.
SF429.B64G53 2006
636.737'4—dc22   2005021156

Note to Parents and Teachers

The Dogs set supports national science standards related to life
science. This book describes and illustrates border collies. The
images support early readers in understanding the text. The
repetition of words and phrases helps early readers learn new
words. This book also introduces early readers to subject-specific
vocabulary words, which are defined in the Glossary section. Early
readers may need assistance to read some words and to use the
Table of Contents, Glossary, Read More, Internet Sites, and Index
sections of the book.

Table of Contents

4

Herding Dogs

Border collies
herd animals.
They keep flocks
of sheep together.

Border collies are
smart dogs who learn fast.
Their owners train them
to play games.

From Puppy to Adult

Puppies are born
in litters of four or more.
Each border collie
has different markings.

Border collie puppies
love to play and learn.
They have lots of energy.

Border collies grow up after about two years. Adults are about as tall as two stairs.

Border Collie Care

Owners need to keep border collies busy. If these dogs are bored, they will find trouble.

Border collies like
to have a job.
Owners can teach them
to herd animals on farms.

Border collies need
dog food every day.
They need to drink
extra water after exercise.

Love and lots of training make border collies happy dogs.

Glossary

energy—the strength to do active things without getting tired

exercise—running, playing, or other movement; border collies need a lot of exercise every day.

flock—a group of animals of one kind that live, travel, or eat together

herd—to keep a group of animals together

litter—a group of animals born at the same time to the same mother

marking—a patch of color

owner—a person who has a dog and takes care of it

train—to teach an animal certain behaviors; border collies can be trained to herd sheep.

Read More

Macken, JoAnn Early. *Puppies.* Let's Read About Pets. Milwaukee: Weekly Reader Early Learning, 2003.

Tagliaferro, Linda. *Dogs and Their Puppies.* Animal Offspring. Mankato, Minn.: Capstone Press, 2004.

Internet Sites

FactHound offers a safe, fun way to find Internet sites related to this book. All of the sites on FactHound have been researched by our staff.

Here's how:

1. Visit *www.facthound.com*
2. Type in this special code **0736853316** for age-appropriate sites. Or enter a search word related to this book for a more general search.
3. Click on the **Fetch It** button.

FactHound will fetch the best sites for you!

Index

Word Count: 126
Grade: 1
Early-Intervention Level: 13

Editorial Credits

Martha E. H. Rustad, editor; Juliette Peters, designer; Jo Miller, photo researcher; Scott Thoms, photo editor

Photo Credits

Bruce Coleman Inc./Jane Burton, 8; Capstone Press/Gary Sundermeyer, 18; Cheryl A. Ertelt, 10; Corbis/Charles Philip Cangialosi, 4; Corbis/Tom Nebbia, 6; Kent Dannen, 14; Lynn M. Stone, 16; Mark Raycroft, 1, 12; Peter Arnold Inc./WWI/J. Baxter, cover; Ron Kimball Stock/Ron Kimball, 20